Sports Day Star

Maverick
Early Readers

'Sports Day Star'
An original concept by Elizabeth Dale
© Elizabeth Dale 2021

Illustrated by Gareth Robinson

Published by MAVERICK ARTS PUBLISHING LTD
Studio 11, City Business Centre, 6 Brighton Road,
Horsham, West Sussex, RH13 5BB
© Maverick Arts Publishing Limited November 2021
+44 (0)1403 256941

A CIP catalogue record for this book is available at the British Library.

ISBN 978-1-84886-826-7

www.maverickbooks.co.uk

This book is rated as: Blue Band (Guided Reading)
It follows the requirements for Phase 4 phonics.
Most words are decodable, and any non-decodable words are familiar,
supported by the context and/or represented in the artwork.

Sports Day Star

by
Elizabeth Dale

illustrated by
Gareth Robinson

It was Sports Day. What fun!

Pip, Pat, Meg and Tom started to hop.

"I can swim deep!" said Pat.

"Look!"

"I can slide well!" said Meg.

"Look!"

"I can dive high!" said Tom.

"Look!"

"I can clap you all!" said Pip.

"You are all so good."

"You will all swim and dive!"
said Big Bill.

Eek!

"You can do it, Pip," said Big Bill.

"Just have fun."

19

Pat, Meg and Tom dived.

They were good.

Good luck, Pip!

"I will do my best," said Pip.

Pip's legs shook.

She was so high up!

Pip started to look down.

But she bent too far.

Pip did a twist and a turn.

"Pip did her best," said Big Bill.

"Pip did the best big dive of all."

Quiz

1. "I can swim _____!" said Pat.
a) high
b) low
c) deep

2. "I can _____ well!" said Meg.
a) glide
b) slide
c) ride

3. "I can dive _____!" said Tom.
a) down
b) high
c) off

4. What does Big Bill tell them to dive for?
a) A big fish
b) A salad
c) A small toy

5. Why did Pip's legs shake?
a) She was tired
b) She was so high up
c) She saw a shark

Turn over for answers

Book Bands for Guided Reading

The Institute of Education book banding system is a scale of colours that reflects the various levels of reading difficulty. The bands are assigned by taking into account the content, the language style, the layout and phonics. Word, phrase and sentence level work is also taken into consideration.

Maverick Early Readers are a bright, attractive range of books covering the pink to white bands. All of these books have been book banded for guided reading to the industry standard and edited by a leading educational consultant.

To view the whole Maverick Readers scheme, visit our website at
www.maverickearlyreaders.com

Or scan the QR code above to view our scheme instantly!

Quiz Answers: 1c, 2b, 3b, 4a, 5b

Pink
Red
Yellow
Blue
Green
Orange
Turquoise
Purple
Gold
White